What Is the Church?

BY JAMES E. FRAZIER

LOYOLAPRESS.
CHICAGO

LOYOLAPRESS.

3441 N. Ashland Avenue
Chicago, Illinois 60657
(800) 621-1008

Acknowledgments:
The Scripture quotations contained herein are from the *New Revised Standard Version Bible*, Catholic edition, copyright © 1993 and 1989 by the Division of Christian Education of the National Council of the Churches of Christ in the U.S.A. Used by permission. All rights reserved.

Song text from "City of God" © 1981, Daniel L. Schutte and New Dawn Music, 5536 NE Hassalo, Portland, OR 97213. All rights reserved. Used with permission.

Song text from "Lord Christ, the Father's Mighty Son" (text by Brian Wren) © 1968, Hope Publishing Co., Carol Stream, IL 60188. All rights reserved. Used by permission.

Song text from "The Church's One Foundation" by Samuel John Stone (1839–1900).

Song text from "O Holy City, Seen of John" from *Hymns of the Christian Life*, Milton S. Littlefield, ed. Copyright © 1910 by Harper & Row.

Cover art: Reprinted from *Clip Art Year B* by Steve Erspamer. Archdiocese of Chicago. Liturgy Training Publications, 1800 North Hermitage Ave., Chicago, IL 60622-1101. 1-800-933-1800. All rights reserved. Used with permission.

ISBN: 0-8294-1110-0

01 02 03 04 05 DataR 7 6 5 4 3

Contents

Introduction

The Church is more wonderful and complex than the colors of a kaleidoscope. We cannot define it with a simple word in a solitary moment, nor can we look at it the same way twice. When we think we understand it, suddenly we turn it to discover its other facets.

At one moment the Church is visible to us, but in the next it becomes invisible. While it is old, it is always new. It is an institution, but it breathes with the breath of the Holy Spirit. The Church is established on holy sites, but it is present everywhere. Everyone is equal in the Church, and yet the Church is a hierarchy that organizes its members into an ordered society. The Church is redeemed, but all of its members are sinners. Like a kaleidoscope, the Church has a mysterious way of eluding definition.

In this book we will look at the many facets of the Church, let the light play on its many aspects, and turn it around and look for ever new views. We may not ever be able to grasp the Church in all its fullness. There will always be something more for us to explore, no matter how young or old we are. Understanding the Church is the task of a lifetime.

1 The Church Is a Building and the People Who Use It

The English word "church"—and the Scottish *kirk* and the German *kirche*—are derived from the Greek word *kyriakon*, meaning "[something] belonging to the Lord." It was originally used of a church building, a building belonging to the Lord. It had a specifically religious meaning.

Another Greek word, however, *ekklesia*, which has given us several English words (like "ecclesial" and "ecclesiastical") that have religious meanings originally had only a secular usage. It denoted the citizens of a self-governing city assembled for legislative or deliberative purposes. The Greek city of Ephesus was such a city (see Acts 19:39). The assembly included only those citizens who had full rights, so the word ekklesia implied the dignity of the members and the legality of the assembly. Even though the word ekklesia referred originally to a secular city, our English words ecclesial and ecclesiastical both have to do with the holy city of the Church.

The English word church implies the meanings of both Greek words, kyriakon and ekklesia: a building belonging to the Lord that is used by God's people. So when we use the word church, sometimes we mean the building and sometimes we mean the people who use the building.

"CHURCH" IN SCRIPTURE

The Greek translators of the Hebrew Old Testament used the word ekklesia to denote the *religious* assembly or congregation of the Israelites, and especially of those in the covenant. The translators were adding their own secular concept of the self-governing assembly to the Israelites' notion of themselves as the citizens of God. In later times the word ekklesia was used to refer also to the local religious assemblies of the Jews who lived outside Jerusalem.

In the Gospels, Jesus uses the word ekklesia when he tells Peter that "on this rock I will build my Church" (Matthew 16:18), and again when he urges one who has been wronged by another to seek redress in the Church (Matthew 18:17).

The local church in Jerusalem was the first to be called an ekklesia. As more and more non-Jews became Christians, local churches were formed in distant cities. Antioch was the earliest and the largest church outside Jerusalem. The Greek Christians in Galatia and in Thessalonica also referred to themselves as churches (Galatians 1:2, 1 Thessalonians 1:1). Because the whole Christian community scattered about the Mediterranean was identified with the church in Jerusalem (Acts 8:1), the word ekklesia was used not only of the church in Jerusalem but of the entire worldwide assembly of the followers of Jesus (1 Corinthians 12:28). All of them, individually and collectively, were the assembly of God's citizens.

HOW "CHURCH" IS USED TODAY

The concept of the Church as the people of God has grown in recent years. Prior to the Second Vatican Council Catholics usually used the word church to refer to the building rather than to themselves.

There is rich sacramental symbolism in using the one word to refer both to the spiritual reality and the material reality. The building stands as a public, civic sign of the holy exchange that takes place on that site between God and the people of God. It is proof that the assembly of God's Church considers that site a holy place.

Scripture makes a similar play on the word "temple." The word usually refers to the splendid temple Solomon built in Jerusalem, but Paul calls the living Church God's temple: "Do you not know that you are God's temple and that God's Spirit dwells in you? . . . For God's temple is holy, and you are that temple" (1 Corinthians 3:16–17). The Church of the living God is the house of God (1 Timothy 3:15). It does not dwell in the heavens, far away and distant from us. Rather, "the home of God is among mortals. He will dwell with them as their God; they will be his peoples" (Revelation 21:3).

In the sacrament of the Eucharist we use the words "the Body of Christ" to refer to the spiritual nourishment we receive at the altar. It was in his human body that Christ accomplished the redemption of the world. By consuming the sacramental body of Christ in the Eucharist, we become the Body of Christ in the world. The body of Christ is the wounded body that hung upon the cross, but it is also the body we receive sacramentally in the Eucharist. In being so nourished, we ourselves become the mystical Body of Christ, which is the Church. The Scriptures and the liturgy both enjoy this kind of verbal richness.

Such ambiguity enables the Church to think of itself as a worldly structure becoming transfigured into the glorified likeness of God. It prevents the Church from becoming so attached to the world that it loses sight of its distant goal. It also prevents the Church from losing touch with the real world. The kingdom of God, after all, is the goal of all our earthly striving.

2 The Church Is a Rich and Wonderful Mystery

In contemporary fiction writing, a mystery is a novel about some puzzling crime. Like a thriller on the movie screen, a mystery involves intrigue and a complex plot that keep the audience in suspense until some secret is revealed at the end. The skill of good mystery writing is to sustain the unexplained until it falls inevitably into view at the end, making sense of all that happened before. The secret is kept secret until the very last page. In a poorly conceived mystery the unexplained becomes obvious too soon in the story; the secret gets out. The perfect mystery is one whose end is missing.

RELIGIOUS MYSTERY

The American love for surprise endings in suspenseful thrillers and murder mysteries complicates our approach to religious mystery. In the Church, mystery is not about suspenseful intrigues manipulated by a divine script writer. God does not play games with us, or treat us like a passive audience. We don't look for thrilling and complex plots in God's dealings with us. Christian mystery is not about surprise endings.

In general Christian terms, a religious mystery is a secret that God reveals to believers. It is God's sharing of the plan of creation and its completion. It is a precious possession given to believers, the secret to living life well, the explanation as to why we should expect to continue to live even after we have died. It is not a secret that God keeps from us.

In the ancient world, the mysteries were the rituals of various secret cults that had become popular in pagan religions before and after the time of Christ. They were nature cults that celebrated the Greek myths of the dying god who returns to life and assures the life cycle of the Earth. Followers of the cult had to be initiated into the mysteries. They enacted the myths ritually and were thus integrated into the renewing cycle of life. They bound themselves by oath not to reveal the mysteries to outsiders. They progressed through various grades of purification to the summit of perfection.

Among the Hebrews, the mysteries were altogether different. In the Old Testament, God's saving designs or purposes were called mysteries (see Wisdom of Solomon 2:22), and sometimes they were revealed to the prophets in dreams (Daniel 2:19, 27–30). The mysteries were God's final decisions about the salvation and judgment that the Hebrews awaited at the end of the world.

The Hebrew mysteries were nothing like the mystery religions of the Graeco-Roman empire, but the Christian mysteries draw elements both from the mystery religions and the Hebrew mysteries.

ELEMENTS OF CHRISTIAN MYSTERY

Christianity celebrates rites and uses terms surprisingly similar to those of the mystery cults. For instance, when catechumens are elected for initiation into the Church, they enter a period of purification and enlightenment. They are given the texts of the Apostles' Creed and the Lord's Prayer as symbols of the tradition, which in the early centuries were "secrets" kept hidden from pagans. Baptism is their ritual initiation. The Eucharist is their enactment of the Lord's last supper, and in the Passover of Christ they enact a saving event that gives them new life. The period after their baptism is called *mystagogy*, when they deepen their new life in Christ by regular attendance at the Eucharist. These features of Christianity resemble practices of the ancient mystery cults.

Christianity also adopted the Hebrew notion of the mysteries of God but with a difference. In the New Testament, generally speaking, a mystery is something that has been revealed as part of God's decisive plan to save the whole world, Jews and non-Jews alike, through the life, death, and resurrection of Jesus. Christ himself is the mystery, and we come to know the mystery in the person of Jesus himself. Divine revelation makes the mystery known to us. Without revelation we can know the parables, but we cannot know the person.

Christ told the disciples that they were entitled to know the secret mysteries of the kingdom of God. The kingdom was either not revealed to outsiders at all, or it was revealed only dimly, or in parables. Outsiders may look but not perceive. They may listen but not understand (Matthew 13:11, Mark 4:11, Luke 8:10).

Because the Church is the Body of Christ, it is also identified as the mystery of Christ. St. Paul said plainly, "This is a great mystery, and I am applying it to Christ and the Church" (Ephesians 5:32).

Paul identifies the mystery as God's plan and decision to redeem the world through the death of Jesus, with all nations made fellow heirs, members of the same body, and sharers in the promise in Christ Jesus (Ephesians 3:3–6). Those who have the mind of Christ understand the wonderful plan of these divine mysteries. All the treasures of wisdom and knowledge are hidden in Christ. Indeed,

God's mystery is Christ himself (Colossians 2:2). The Church is the avenue through which the mystery of God's saving will and the riches of holy wisdom are revealed to us (Ephesians 3:10).

Paul described the wisdom of God as a mystery that confounds human wisdom and is unknown to the world's rulers. It was revealed to the apostles through the Spirit and is intelligible only to those endowed with the Spirit (1 Corinthians 2:1–16). To them God reveals the mystery of his will, which is to gather all things in Christ (Ephesians 1:9–10). The apostles are the guardians of these mysteries (1 Corinthians 4:1), which were unknown to former ages. St. Paul reminds us that it is not enough to merely understand the secrets of the mysteries. We must also have love (1 Corinthians 13:2).

A mystery revealed is not necessarily a mystery understood. Although the mystery of God's love is plain to our eyes and ears (which is why it appeals even to young children), it is so rich and multileveled that it engages the thoughtful and inquisitive believer for a lifetime.

There is no end to our contemplation of the paschal mystery of Christ, the Lamb whose death won victory for us over death. We can never exhaust the mystery of a God who became human and died, and whose mother was a virgin. He was the priest of his own sacrifice, a servant and yet a king, who ascended from Earth but is somehow still present to us and promises to come again.

Artists and musicians are models for the contemplation of mystery in the Church. Through the craft of architects, artists, poets, and musicians we have precious glimpses of the mystery of Christ. These visionaries have contemplated the mystery, and have designed the churches, painted the frescoes, written the texts, composed the melodies, chiseled the statues, and glazed the windows that we use in our own contemplation. Thanks in part to the prophetic vision of these artists, the mystery that was hidden for ages is now revealed to the saints, and the mystery is "Christ in you" (Colossians 1:26–27).

Through the mysteries of God, the relationship that Christ has with the Church is like a marriage union. The relationship is itself a great mystery (Ephesians 5:22–32) and is the effect of God's plan for salvation. Modern theology has called this union of Christ and the Church a mystical union.

THE MYSTICAL UNION

The mystical nature of Christ's union with the Church derives from Christ's enduring presence among us, particularly in the sacraments and in the word. The sacraments and the word proclaimed in the Church are tokens of the relationship between Christ and the Church. They are the glances and glimpses, the loving winks exchanged at important moments in the relationship between Christ and the Church. They are the means through which the fullness of Christ is communicated to us.

When Christ is in us, we are also in Christ. The union between us and Christ is what makes the Church a mystery. It is a mystical union of the Body of Christ, with Christ himself as head. The Church is the mystery of our encounter with Christ.

Those who respond to God's word enter into this mystery. We become members of Christ's body and are intimately united with him. We don't join the Church the same way we join a society or sign up our kids for the scouts. The Church is not a special interest group nor is it an easy way to pass off the religious education of our kids. We don't enter the Church the way we join a bowling league, Phi Beta Kappa, or a country club: We need a certain skill to join the league, a high IQ to join the society, and lots of money to join the club.

Those who are called into the Church are called into the life of Christ communicated to believers through participation in the Church's sacramental life. Those who respond to God's call to become members of the Church can only persevere in the grace of God. Membership is not conditioned on one's birth, upbringing, education, or financial status. Some people find it more difficult to respond to the call to enter the mystery of the Church, but no one is excluded because of personal circumstances.

Many people do not respond to the call to enter the Church. Some do so out of ignorance, or misinformation, or because they were not exposed to the Church as youngsters. Others do not heed the call because of what they perceive as hypocrisy in Christians they know. Others think that the Church resists scientific research, or perpetuates a ghetto mentality isolated from mainstream culture.

In *The Church in the Modern World*, the Second Vatican Council teaches that Christians are sometimes responsible for keeping people out of the Church. When they are careless about their instruction in the faith, or when they misrepresent its teaching, they conceal God from the view of others. When they fail in their religious, moral, or social obligations, they give false witness about Christ. When they misinterpret the plan of God for the world, they cloud the mysteries that God long ago revealed to all peoples. The Second Vatican Council taught that believers are sometimes responsible for atheism.

The mystery of the Church is for everyone, no matter the circumstances of their birth. Indeed, the mystery of the Church is richer for its having been revealed to the rich diversity of all the citizens of Earth.

3 The Church Is One, Holy, Catholic, and Apostolic

In its earliest days, the Church was little more than a humble group of fishermen, some tax collectors, a zealot, a couple of impetuous brothers, one who doubted, another who betrayed and then committed suicide, and another who denied the charismatic, roving preacher named Jesus. They had no thought of themselves as an institution, and they spent no time defining their teachings or setting up organizational structures.

As time went on, the communities of Jesus' disciples grew in their understanding of themselves and became more well defined. The Scriptures show that as the Church dealt with internal disputes, decisions were made that helped to establish the character of the Church.

The Church saw that there could be only *one* Body of Christ, not several. It decided that non-Jews could become Christians without having to become Jews first. This meant that the Church saw itself not as exclusive but as *catholic* and worldwide. It held that because the Church came to be by God it must be *holy.* And it held that because its teaching came from the apostles, and was handed on from them, it had to remain faithful to *apostolic* teaching.

These characteristic marks, or notes, of the Church were first enumerated in the Nicene Creed, which was issued in 325 AD by the council of bishops who met in Nicaea. The creed declares the Church to be one, holy, catholic, and apostolic. It is used regularly in the eucharistic worship of the historic Churches, those in union with Rome as well as the Orthodox Churches of the East. It was first used in eucharistic worship in Antioch in the fifth century but was not adopted at Rome until 1014. The Nicene Creed has been widely accepted in modern times as a proposed basis for the unity of the Roman Church with the Orthodox Churches and with those in the West that separated at the time of the sixteenth-century Reformation.

During the Reformation, extreme diversity in doctrine, worship, and government stretched the Church's identity beyond limits that were acceptable at the time. The four notes of the Church were used by Roman Catholic theologians to discern the true Church from rival claims of other Christian bodies. Some declared themselves so deeply at odds with the tenets of Rome that they could no longer be considered one with her. They were said to be outside the one, holy, catholic, and apostolic Church. Rome declared them heretics or schismatics and pronounced them to be deprived of salvation by virtue of their separation from the one, true Church.

With the Second Vatican Council (1962–1965), Rome adopted a more scriptural view of the Church, one that accepted all who have been baptized by water and the Spirit as members of the Body of Christ and, therefore, heirs of salvation.

THE CHURCH IS ONE

We can discern the oneness of the Church when all its members share in the sacraments of baptism, confirmation, and the Eucharist. Virtually all Christians of all denominations are baptized, confirmed, and commune in the Lord.

Jesus described himself as the shepherd of his flock. He gave his life for his sheep. When there are sheep outside his fold he goes to lead them in so that they can become part of his own flock. He desires that all be part of the one flock under the one shepherd (John 10:1–10).

In the earliest times the doctrine of the visible unity of the Church was accepted everywhere. Jesus had committed his flock to Peter, appointing him its shepherd (John 21:15–17). The Church thought of its unity as being safeguarded by its foundation in Peter (Matthew 16:18). Jesus prayed that his followers be one as he and his Father are one, and that his followers may be united with him and his Father (John 17:20–21).

The local church in Jerusalem was the parent church of all the other local churches described in the New Testament. It represented the unity of the early churches. Peter was the leader of the church in Jerusalem immediately after Jesus' ascension.

Jerusalem sent representatives to investigate conditions in other churches (Acts 15:3), and met in assembly to resolve questions referred to it by other churches (Acts 15:22).

At the same time, Paul used the word ekklesia in the plural, signifying that the separate local churches were equal. Unity within each of the local congregations was a sign of the Church's larger unity. Paul, however, struggled to preserve the unity of the individual churches.

Challenges to Unity

The local churches had suffered division because some members claimed an allegiance to Paul, while others claimed an allegiance to Apollos or Cephas or Christ. Paul wrote to them to remind them that they were all baptized into Christ, and that it was Christ alone who had died for them. Their quarrels and rifts divided the Body of Christ (1 Corinthians 11:18–19, Galatians 1:6–9, 1 John 2:18–19).

Various movements also developed elsewhere within the Church to challenge its unity. In the earliest of these disputes, the Church had to decide whether its unity was at risk by allowing Greeks to become Christian without first becoming Jews. The Church decided that its unity was not threatened by having both Jews and non-Jews as members.

A few centuries later, a group of believers held that Christ had only one nature, a divine nature. In their view it demeaned Christ to think of him as being human. Because the Church had always thought of Christ as both divine and human, those who held the contrary view were declared to be outside the Church. The Church could not remain one if some believers held the belief that Christ had two natures while others believed he had only one.

Another dispute took place during the Roman persecutions. Between the years 250 and 320 the Church suffered from systematic persecution by the Roman state. The Romans demanded that bishops surrender the Scriptures and liturgical books. Bishops who turned them over to the state were considered traitors. When the persecutions lapsed, the Church had a difficult time deciding what to do with those who had betrayed the Church. Some thought that they should be permanently excluded from the Church. Others thought that they should be readmitted on the condition that they do penance for the rest of their lives.

As a consequence of these disputes, a theology of the Church gradually developed, making it easier to determine whether a group was one with the Church or separate from it.

Different Forms of Church Develop

After the fourth century, the Church took varying forms as it spread from Rome into France, Germany, Britain, and Ireland. These churches had different models for spirituality, worship, and Church government.

Monasticism produced still other models of Church life that coexisted with the prevailing forms. In themselves these variations in piety, worship, and government enriched the Church's diversity without jeopardizing its unity.

The Church has always taken a flexible view of unity. It has allowed varieties in Church government, in piety, in worship, in spirituality, and in the way it relates to the world and to civil governments. We see this flexibility most clearly in the unity of the various historic rites. The Catholic Churches of the Byzantine, Melchite, Maronite, Coptic, and Roman rites are one in their faith, even though their government, their worship, and their spiritualities vary considerably from one another. Many of them allow their clergy to marry, while priests in the Roman rite are not permitted to marry. Even this contentious issue does not constitute division in the Body of Christ.

The story is quite different for the Church of Rome and the Eastern Orthodox Churches. For many centuries they had been at odds with each other. Sometimes the issues were more political than religious. In 1054 each Church declared itself to be the one, true, historic Church, and each declared the other to be in schism.

One issue separating the East from the West today is the date for celebrating Easter. The Eastern Churches observe Easter according to the old Julian calendar. The Western Churches follow the Gregorian calendar, which is in use throughout all the modern world. There have been attempts to agree on a common date, so that at least the observance of Easter would be a sign of unity among Catholics and Orthodox.

Prior to the Second Vatican Council, Roman Catholics had a tangible sense of their unity worldwide. They could worship anywhere in the world, hear the same Latin texts, and recognize the same ceremony they saw in their home parishes. Unity in the Catholic Church was thought to depend on the strict uniformity of worship everywhere. The uniformity of Catholic worship and life provided a great sense of security.

American Catholicism

While there were a few early Catholic settlements in what is now the continental United States, most of the 13 colonies were staunchly Protestant. The Spanish settlements in the Southwest and in Florida, and the French settlements in Louisiana, were far removed from the activity in the colonies on the East Coast.

With the influx of immigrants from Catholic Europe to America in the nineteenth century, a vigorous anti-Catholicism led to bigotry and even riots. Catholics were seen as a threat to American life and thought. How could any loyal American declare allegiance to a foreign head of state like the pope in the Vatican?

Some bishops and cardinals publicly urged Catholics to become active members of American society, participating fully in the democratic ways of their new homeland. Today Roman Catholics have entered the mainstream of American civic, cultural, and corporate life and exercised strong leadership in setting its course.

The challenge to the unity of American Catholicism today comes not from outside but from within. What does it mean to be Catholic in the modern world? Are American Catholics all that different from their neighbors who belong to other Christian denominations? Liberal Catholics will answer these questions in one way. Conservative Catholics will answer them in quite another way.

Diversity and Unity

The Second Vatican Council authorized the use of vernacular languages and welcomed cultural influences on Catholic worship, and today there is considerable variation in worship styles, not only from country to country but from parish to parish, all across the United States.

North American parishes have developed "personalities" that attract members across geographic boundary lines. Some will attend a church for its contemporary music while others will go where there is good preaching or strong outreach to the homeless and hungry. Sometimes the charism of the pastor is a factor in building an attractive, vibrant community. No matter where one becomes a member, Christ is the same everywhere, and the sacraments are equally valid in them all, whether they be administered solemnly in a noble cathedral, or informally behind a storefront window. The diversity of parish personalities does not put the Church's unity at risk.

A Catholic Vietnamese family that emigrates to the United States is entitled to worship in a parish where the word of God is proclaimed in a language they can understand, and where their cultural traditions can flourish. Their use of the Vietnamese language at worship does not threaten the unity of Roman Catholicism. They are in full communion with all other American Roman Catholics, with Hispanic Catholics, and with Ojibwe Catholics who use the language of their native American forebears to express their faith at Mass. Their unity in the one faith transcends all their cultural differences.

Extreme diversity today, however, has forced the Church to look closely at the limits of diversity. How diverse can the Church be before its essential unity is threatened? Experiments on left and right have posed particular challenges to Roman Catholic unity in the United States.

Ecumenism

The faith life of Catholics across much of the United States today has much in common with that of non-Catholics, much more than it did before the Second Vatican Council. The modern ecumenical movement has tried to restore Christian unity at a level that transcends differences in creed, ritual, and Church government.

The unity of the Church in New Testament times is the unity to which we aspire today. In the earliest centuries the diversity of practice from one city to the next only strengthened the Church's unity. The fact that the church in Antioch was not identical to the church in Corinth did not threaten the Church's unity.

The movement to restore unity has never been stronger than it is in our century. Today's ecumenical movement continues the efforts begun in the eighteenth and nineteenth centuries when an evangelical revival crossed national and denominational lines.

In 1960 Pope John XXIII met with the archbishop of Canterbury as an expression of the Vatican's changing attitude about cooperation and reunion. And in 1965 Pope Paul VI met with the Ecumenical Patriarch Athenagoras to lift their mutual excommunications of each other's Churches. These overtures to the separated Churches of the West and the East were the Vatican's first significant steps toward eventual reunion.

Non-Roman Catholics were invited to attend the Second Vatican Council as observers, and in 1964 the council promulgated the *Decree on Ecumenism.* The decree represented a significant break with tradition. It declared that the restoration of unity among all Christians was one of the principal concerns of the Second Vatican Council. It acknowledged that both sides had made mistakes leading to the regrettable separations of previous centuries. It said that those born into the separated communities cannot be charged with the sin of separation. It declared the separated bodies to be ecclesial communities. And it declared that anyone who believes in Christ and is properly baptized enjoys some communion, though imperfectly, with the Catholic Church. In other words, the Catholic Church said that all who have been justified by faith through the waters of baptism are incorporated into Christ and can therefore be saved.

Every year Churches of all denominations observe a week of prayer for Christian unity. Services of common worship take place in the week that begins on the Feast of the Confession of St. Peter on January 18 and ends on the Feast of the Conversion of St. Paul on January 25.

This text by the contemporary hymn writer Brian Wren represents an impassioned plea of all the Churches seeking unity:

Lord Christ, the Father's mighty Son,
Whose work upon the cross was done
To give and receive,
Make all our scattered Churches one,
That the world may believe.

To make us one your prayers were said,
To make us one you broke the bread
For all to receive;
Its pieces scatter us instead:
How can others believe?

We will not question or refuse
The way you work, the means you choose,
The pattern you weave;
But reconcile our warring views,
That the world may believe.

THE CHURCH IS HOLY

God told Israel, "I am the Lord your God; sanctify yourselves therefore, and be holy, for I am holy" (Leviticus 11:44). Isaiah the prophet saw angels attending the Lord upon the throne. They called to one another, saying, "Holy, holy, holy is the Lord of hosts; the whole Earth is full of his glory" (Isaiah 6:1–3).

Through his own life and death, Christ hallowed the Church. He cleansed it in his own blood, sealed it in the

Spirit at baptism, and made it holy. It has no stain or wrinkle (Ephesians 5:22–32).

St. Paul described the Church as a holy temple of the Lord, with the members incorporated into its structure (Ephesians 2:20). He called the members of the Church saints who are hallowed in Christ, called to be holy (1 Corinthians 1:2), the holy ones of God (Colossians 3:12).

Jesus warned his followers that discipleship involved personal attachment to him, even at the cost of their attachment to the world, their friends, and their family. Their separation from the world could even lead to an ultimate separation through death (Matthew 4:18–22, 10:34; Mark 1:16–20, 8:34–38; Luke 5:1–11, 12:51–53).

The New Testament does not teach that flight from the world leads to holiness. It does, however, teach that as long as the world is unrepentant, it is sinful (John 12:31–36, 14:30, 18:36), and that an inordinate attachment to the things of the world is harmful.

In the early centuries, the Church viewed martyrdom as the ultimate form of holiness. Martyrdom was the greatest sacrifice that a Christian could make in imitation of the sacrifice of Christ on the cross. After the persecutions ended and Christians no longer had to suffer for choosing to follow Christ, holiness was seen in the symbolic death of the body in the asceticism and purity of monasticism.

MONASTICISM

Monasticism began as a way of leading the life of holiness in greater security than is possible in the busy world. It originated in Egypt in the fourth century with St. Anthony, who gave away his possessions and became a hermit, devoting himself to a life of asceticism. St. Benedict later wrote the famous rule that described the life of a monastic community. For several centuries the Benedictine rule was a principal form of religious life in the Catholic Church.

The chief aim of the monastic life is to pursue personal holiness by living the three disciplines of poverty, chastity, and obedience in a particularly deliberate way. The monk or nun usually lives in a cloister and has little contact with the outside world. There are many orders of religious men and women, however, who take similar vows but are actively involved with lay Catholics in teaching, nursing, and social work. In some orders of men the members are priests who live in community and staff parishes. In others the members are not ordained. They are called brothers, and they often engage in teaching and nursing ministries, or in social work. Communities of active religious women have historically dedicated themselves primarily to teaching and nursing. In our day many sisters work for social justice and peace. All religious orders, whether cloistered or active, pursue personal holiness with particular zeal.

Holiness and the Laity

Simplicity of life; purity of mind, heart, and body; and responsiveness to the needs of the world should characterize the lives of all who are baptized into Christ, not just priests and vowed religious. Catholic laity have traditionally pursued holiness of life by imitating and adapting the devotional practices of clergy and religious. They held up the life of the priest or religious as the model for themselves as well.

The way of holiness for lay Christians, however, is accessible to mothers and dads in their lives of choice, and to aunts and uncles, to our kids and our cousins, to everybody who attends school or works at blue-collar or white-collar jobs. We have all been called to holiness, no matter what our circumstances in life may be.

The overwhelming majority of the saints who have feast days on the Church's liturgical calendar were priests, bishops, popes, or vowed religious. After Mary and Joseph, very few were lay persons, and most of these were kings and queens. Among the few laity on the Roman calendar who were not royalty are St. Isidore the farmer, St. Thomas More, St. Maria Goretti, the native American Blessed Kateri Tekakwitha, the Korean martyr St. Paul Chong Hasang, and the Filipino St. Lawrence Ruiz. Of the 117 martyrs canonized with St. Andrew Dung-Lac in 1988 by Pope John Paul II, 59 were laity.

The Bible calls all people to holiness in the context of their particular station in life. Unlike priests and sisters, Catholic laity have the commitments of family, home, and workplace through which they attain their own holiness.

The Second Vatican Council proposed an outline of holiness for the laity. It taught that the holiness of the Church manifests itself through various states in life (lay, religious, and priestly) and that the Trinity is the fountain of all holiness. The laity foster their holiness and ever-deepening unity through the liturgical and sacramental life of the Church. The Church acclaims God's holiness at every celebration of the Eucharist.

The council taught that Christians should be completely involved in the world, proving their faith in God, and fulfilling their own vocation. They should use and enjoy the world with detachment in order to fulfill their responsibilities and to safeguard against the abuse of creation. Christians should heal the world of its abuses and injustices in order to continue Christ's redemption of the universe. They should transform the world into what it is capable of being, and discover all that is noble and good. Christians consecrate the world to God in Christ.

This kind of holiness impresses upon lay men and women the meaning of their own existence and their dignity in a world that often spurns human values. Their holiness takes many rich and diverse forms.

THE CHURCH IS CATHOLIC

The word "catholic" is commonly used in three different ways, and it is hard to distinguish their sometimes overlapping meanings, or to know which use is intended. Above all, the word catholic means that Christianity is open to all people everywhere, everywhere on the globe, regardless of their race, their nationality, or their culture. It is not necessary to become an Italian citizen, for instance, before being baptized a Roman Catholic.

The word catholic also is used to describe a formal style of ceremonial worship and a type of Church government that involves an ordained hierarchy and apostolic ministry. In this sense Roman Catholicism is catholic but so are many Episcopal and Lutheran churches. Baptists would not ordinarily consider themselves catholic in this sense.

When the word is capitalized, Catholic refers to all Churches in union with the pope. Roman Catholics, therefore, are Catholic, but Maronites, for instance, are Catholic, too.

The first Christians were Jews. Their faith in Christ did not isolate them from their Jewish families or from regular Jewish worship. They were faithful to Jewish law and to the practice of Judaism. As more and more non-Jews became Christian, however, the Church became less attached to Judaism and to Jerusalem, and took on a more universal character. This led to increasing flexibility in the Church's understanding of itself. As it became more universal in its geographical reach, the Church at the same time became more catholic in its identity. Greeks who wanted to become Christian, for instance, were not forced to become Jews first, or to follow Jewish Law. A Church that calls itself catholic is open to the people of all nations everywhere.

By the time the Church had spread over most of the known world and was being challenged by various heretical movements, it had already come to consider itself as being catholic.

The Local Church

In order for the Church to be catholic, it must also be local. It must exist in real communities where people known to each other meet regularly in the name of Christ for prayer, for the breaking of bread, fellowship, and for the communal sharing of their resources. We find small units of the Church in old center-city parishes, in large thriving parishes in the suburbs, and in simpler parishes in small rural towns. All are real manifestations of the universal, catholic Church. The Church cannot be catholic without them.

The local parish is a geographical area that has a church at its heart where the parishioners gather to worship. Catholics who live within that area are members of that parish. Owing to the diversity of Catholic life and thought in North America today, some households prefer to be members of a parish other than their local geographic parish. They travel a distance to attend a church where the worship or the program is more to their liking.

For similar reasons, national parishes have been established for those whose language and culture make it difficult for them to assemble and worship in their closest geographic parishes.

During the decades of European immigration to the United States in the nineteenth and early twentieth centuries, many national parishes were established where German, Italian, Irish, and Polish Catholics could be served by priests who spoke their language in the church, and by sisters who could teach their children in the schools. Immigration in our own day has created a similar need for Asian and Hispanic parishes, for people from Vietnam or Latin America. Many African Americans and native Americans also prefer to worship in their own communities of faith.

The Domestic Church

Every local church consists of a number of households or nuclear families. The household is a domestic church, a household of faith. It is the smallest unit in which the life of Christ is manifest and lived in community. Sufficient numbers of households warrant establishing a local congregation and incorporating as a parish.

Parents are to nurture their children in Christian values and form them in the mind of Christ. Children brought up in a domestic church will develop a sense they are part of a community that loves them and to which they have some social responsibility. In the family they receive their earliest instruction in the faith. Parents have primary responsibility for the Christian education of their children, even after more formal schooling is passed along to professional educators. The family household is a model both for the parish and for the larger Church worldwide.

The earliest Christian assemblies met in the homes of their members. They did not have large, imposing buildings. The image of the fish came to symbolize these humble and modest meetings. Like the loaf of bread and the cup of wine, the fish reminded the early believers of the simple meals that Jesus shared with his disciples on a hillside, in their homes, or on a lakeshore. The image of the stylized fish has become common in our own day as a symbol not only of meals shared in the name of the Lord but of the humble domestic foundation that the worldwide Catholic Church has in the simplest family household.

THE CHURCH IS APOSTOLIC

The Church is apostolic because its authority derives from the authority of the apostles, and because the truth of its teaching is ensured through the succession of that authority through the bishops of the Church.

When Jesus told Peter that he is the rock upon which the Church is built, he indicated the peculiar place Peter would hold in the assembly of his followers. The Catholic Church has always understood this foundation in Peter to be Jesus' promise of the Church's permanence through the apostles and their bishop successors.

The spread of the Church across the known world was the result of the missionary activity by the apostles. The apostles established and led the local churches in Jerusalem, for instance, and in other cities. The Jerusalem community sent the apostle Barnabas to Antioch (Acts 11:22). St. Mark is considered the founder of the Church in Alexandria, Egypt. St. James was the apostle in Jerusalem after Peter left. The apostle Thomas took the Gospel to India, and the Christians in Malabar hold him as their founder. St. Peter, of course, became the apostle to the Church in Rome.

St. Paul was not one of the original 12 apostles, and yet the Church calls him the apostle to the Gentiles. His dramatic conversion determined his particular view of the Church and resulted in his missionary work to spread the Gospel and establish Christian communities. His conversion led to his life as an apostle.

In a similar way, St. Patrick is called the apostle to Ireland, and Sts. Cyril and Methodius are the apostles to the Slavs. They were the leaders of the earliest Christian mission to their respective countries.

Diversity of Apostleship

The apostolic ministry of the Church is handed down from one generation to another through what is called *apostolic succession*. The series of bishops who have succeeded one another since the apostles ensures the Church's apostolic authority. The bishops perform the functions of the apostles, their commission is the same as that of the apostles, they succeed one another in a lineage that is traced to the apostles, and at their episcopal ordination they inherit the power of the Holy Spirit to perform their apostolate faithfully.

Apostleship, however, belongs not only to the great apostles and to their bishop successors but to all members of the Body of Christ as well. The Church is apostolic not only because it is founded upon the faith, the teaching, and the missionary activity of the apostles but because all whose lives have been turned around in Christ have the calling of an apostle. They are to spread the Gospel so that Christ is embodied in the world.

The apostolate among the laity takes many forms. The responsible raising of children in the Church is an apostolic activity. Hospitality to the homeless and the hungry is an apostolic activity. So is the cloistered life of prayer. And so is the defense of Christian values in the marketplace and in government. Whatever we do to help build the city of God among the peoples of the Earth is an apostolic activity.

INFALLIBILITY

Jesus told his disciples that the Spirit of truth will guide them into all the truth (John 16:13). He also told Peter that the Church was built upon a rock and that the gates of hell would not prevail against it (Matthew 16:18). The Roman Catholic Church and other Churches as well have understood these words of Jesus to mean that the Church cannot err in its teaching of revealed truths. They believe the Church is infallible.

The Churches, however, do not all agree on a definition of infallibility. Some Churches believe infallibility resides in the revealed word of God alone, not in any later teachings by the Church and not in the bishops or popes. Many Churches hold that only those doctrines and truths accepted by all the ancient, historic branches of the Church are infallible. Some Churches accept as infallible only the definitions of the ecumenical councils of the first few centuries of the Church.

At the First Vatican Council in 1870, the Roman Catholic Church declared that the pope was infallible when he defines a doctrine of faith or morals as part of the deposit of divine revelation handed down from apostolic tradition. These teachings are to be believed by the whole Church because the Church cannot err in teaching revealed truth.

The First and Second Vatican Councils also held that when the entire body of bishops are in union with the pope in teaching some aspect of the deposit of revelation, they teach with the same infallibility. This holds whether or not the bishops are assembled in an ecumenical council.

In the view of the Roman Catholic Church, papal infallibility is based on the apostolic character of our living faith. So in making formal pronouncements about what the Church believes, the pope and the bishops are to refer to the living apostolic faith of their respective churches.

It is not by some miracle or clairvoyance that doctrine is revealed and defined in the Church. Rather it is by the grace of God, who preserves the Church from error. Since salvation in Christ is God's decisive victory in the world, the reality of the Church is structured on the eternal truth of God's loving action on our behalf.

4 The Church Enjoys the Real Presence of God Yet Waits to See God Face to Face

Doubt is an important part of a mature, living faith. It comes with growing up and being inquisitive about the world. As children we are not likely to challenge authority or to doubt what we are taught about God or the Church. At adolescence, however, we begin to question the teachings of the Church and to wonder if they aren't just meaningless platitudes. Findings from the sciences and sociology start to seem compelling. Poetry and nature suffice for worship, and religion starts to seem irrelevant to a comfortable life. If faith is to be a real part of our lives, we have to struggle honestly with its meaning and ask difficult questions. Doubt is inevitable.

Ultimately all we want is a deep and abiding confidence that some things in life are dependable and trustworthy, even when everything else changes around us. We want to know that despite the fast pace of our lives, and the speed with which modern values change, we are assured of a certain stability in the matters that are most important to us.

THE STABILITY OF FAITH

It was easy for earlier generations of Catholics to learn the truths of their faith and to depend on their remaining true for a lifetime. The *Baltimore Catechism* provided young

Catholics with answers to the important questions about their faith. In catechism classes they memorized the answers and appreciated the faith as stable and dependable.

Ever since the Second Vatican Council opened its dialogue with the modern world, Catholics have learned that certain aspects of the faith that they once thought unchangeable were in fact conditioned by time and space. They discovered that abstinence from meat on Fridays, for instance, was not essential to faith, and that it might even be irrelevant in vegetarian cultures.

When so many changes were unleashed upon them after the Council, particularly in the way they worship, many Catholics felt the loss of assurances that they had always enjoyed. They found themselves doubting the authority of the priests and sisters who had once taught them security in matters of faith. They doubted the wisdom of the council. Some have come to doubt the teachings of their bishops and the encyclicals of the popes, declaring them out of touch with the real world.

The life of faith is always difficult in times of transition, whether the transition is an internal one in our personal lives, or an external one in the changes in society. The stability of our faith sometimes has nothing to depend on other than a sense of God's presence.

SCRIPTURE AND FAITH

The Gospels show us just how faith can falter in difficult times. The apostles had lost Jesus. He had been murdered by the Roman soldiers. Thomas doubted Jesus could be alive again, despite what the other apostles were saying. Thomas said he would not believe Jesus was alive without actually seeing for himself. Thomas is a model for us precisely in his doubting.

Many Christians can trust their feelings to provide some assurance that they are living lives worthy of the Gospel, and that they have found favor with God. They depend on Mass and other devotions to give them feelings of confidence in the Lord. When they read the Scriptures and when they pray in private, they enjoy the presence of God, and they have the sense that they have been "found" or "saved" by God. This is spiritual comfort for them in the midst of life's ups and downs.

Some Christians are skeptical that their feelings convey anything of spiritual importance. Many of the saints experienced "dry" periods or the "dark night of the soul," when they felt God was distant from them, or as if God had even abandoned them. Such feelings can seem like a spiritual condemnation. Some describe it as a living hell.

The Scriptures describe what it is like to experience the absence or the anger of God. For instance, in all the suffering that he endured, the innocent man Job struggled to understand why innocent people should suffer. In the entire Book of Esther, a narrative about how a Jewish woman was able to save her fellow Jews, the name of God is never even mentioned. And dying on the cross, Christ cried out, asking why God had abandoned him. The Scriptures help us to understand the feeling of God's absence when life seems to be failing us.

The Scriptures also tell us that we can trust the assurances that faith gives us. We know by faith, for instance, that not even death can separate us from God's love (Romans 8:38–39). In other words, when our health fails us and we feel ourselves becoming isolated from the world and our loved ones, especially at death, even then we have God's loving companionship. When Jesus realized that his disciples were fearful about his departure, he promised them he would not leave them without comfort but would send a Comforter (John 14:18, 26).

THE EUCHARIST

In addition to the promises of Scripture, Catholics have the ministry of the bishop, the priest, and the deacon as evidence of God's comforting presence in the Church. Through these ordained ministers, Catholics also have the sacraments to assure them that their faith will survive all turmoil, transition, and doubt. The sacraments are comfortable words and assuring signs that God is with us. For all the baptized, the Eucharist, above all, endures as God's presence among us. It will not leave us comfortless.

The Catholic Church believes God's presence in the Eucharist to be *real* because its reality as God-among-us does not depend on us. It does not depend on our minds or our feelings to make it *seem* real. It does not go away from us when we feel spiritually alone. The sacrament is not just a memory or a reminder of Jesus. It is not something that we imagine, or something there one day but gone the next, as if it depended on our mental states or on our own faithfulness. In the Eucharist, God is really present, to be seen and touched and consumed, even when we have willfully turned away. The reservation of the Eucharist in the tabernacle enables Catholics to trust the Church as a place where God is always present, even when everything else seems doubtful.

The Church can lay claim to God's presence because at a particular time in history Christ took flesh in the Incarnation. Born of a woman and the Holy Spirit, the Son of God lived on Earth and was involved in the affairs of the world. The Jesus of Bethlehem, who ascended into heaven 40 days after he rose from the dead, is the same Christ present in the Eucharist. That presence is the Church's precious possession.

Those who followed Jesus believed him to be the Messiah promised by the prophets and anticipated by the Jews. Those who choose not to follow him are still awaiting their Messiah. The Jews doubt the reality of Christ as the Messiah. Similarly, skeptics and agnostics look at the world around them and see evidence that a savior has yet to come.

THE MEANING OF ADVENT

The season of Advent in the Church's calendar is difficult to explain and defend. If Christians believe that their Messiah has already come, what is the purpose of Advent? Why observe a season that puts us in a time of suspenseful anticipation of a Savior that we believe has already come? What are we waiting for if Christ has already come?

Skeptics and agnostics have a good case when they point to the suffering and injustice in the world. If Christ has come, they say, why is there still so much evil in the world? Racism is everywhere, a holocaust obliterates millions of people, refugees are forced from their homes to live in squalid camps, rampant commercialism turns human beings into consuming objects, traditional family values are in decline, and the poor are the means of material profit by international corporations. If a good God gave his only Son to save the world from the forces of death and evil, why is the world still such a mess? It looks like Christ has still not come.

When the Church observes the season of Advent, it enters into solidarity with the Jews, and with all the world's skeptics and agnostics. Advent puts us in wait alongside all non-believers who claim that the Savior has not come and who point to the state of the world as proof. We admit with them that there is still much work to be done, even though we insist that Christ has already come and redeemed the world. During Advent the Church accepts evil, corruption, and death as proof that Christ is not yet all in all. Advent is the Church's admission that when the kingdom of God is finally established on Earth, we will recognize it by another coming of Christ.

In the meantime we know the feeling of being Jewish and of waiting for a deliverer. We live in solidarity with skeptics and agnostics. We know the absence of God and the darkness of night. We know we have no choice but to wait even though we've been assured that Christ is already present among us. We remember the unbearable feeling of spiritual abandonment.

At every Eucharist the Church prays for the needs of the world. Like Advent, these intercessions place us in wait with all the world for the coming of the kingdom, when life will at last be victorious over death. When Christ comes again, there will be no needs to be prayed for, because Christ will be all in all.

In the Church we know the real presence of God, and we know God's painful absence. The spiritual needs that we all experience are like a personal Advent, and they come at any time and any place. They do not wait for the four weeks before Christmas. God seems to go from us in our efforts at prayer, and in our labors in the world.

In the Church's proclamation of the word, however, God enters into our life, and in the Eucharist we return to the joy of God's real presence. Our spiritual darkness, our doubts in the faith, and our fear of God's distance find comfort in the words of Scripture and in the Eucharist.

Our life in the Church is one long Advent until Christ comes again in glory. On that day, when Advent comes to an end at last, all those tokens of Christ's presence—the proclamation of the word, the sacraments, the ministry of bishops and priests, even the blessed Eucharist—all will become unnecessary. With a beatific vision of the face of God, what more could we ever want or need?

5 The Church Is Both Visible and Invisible

The Church on Earth is the visible Church of the living. Those who have died in Christ constitute the invisible Church of the faithful departed. They who enjoy the beatific vision of God face to face are called the Church triumphant. They are also invisible to us.

THE VISIBLE CHURCH

As the visible Body of Christ on Earth, the Church is a visible society of the members of Christ. We can see the Church in its churches and schools, in its diocesan offices and charitable agencies, and in the hierarchy of its baptized members: the laity and the ordained. The organization of its leadership is a manifestation of the visible Church. The Church gathers around its bishops and priests, and is assisted by its deacons in celebrating the sacred mysteries and responding to the needs of the world. The Church's bishops are organized by regional conferences that allow them to exercise their episcopal ministry more effectively. The most visible manifestation of the Church is Vatican City, where the pope presides over the Catholic Church worldwide.

We can observe the operation of the Church through the participation of its members in the seven visible sacraments of baptism, confirmation, Eucharist, reconciliation, matrimony, holy orders, and the anointing of the sick. The sacraments initiate, nurture, reconcile, and organize the

Church's visible membership. They are the visible signs of the Church's life in an invisible God and of one's union with the visible Church. Our participation in the sacramental life of the Church is proof of our connection with the visible Church and its invisible God.

It sometimes becomes necessary for someone to be excluded from the visible life of the Church because of heretical beliefs or notorious immoral actions. Jesus himself allowed that excommunication may be necessary. "If the offender refuses to listen even to the Church, let such a one be to you as a Gentile and a tax collector" (Matthew 18:17). St. Paul told the Church in Corinth that there had to be factions among them because that was the only way to determine who is genuine (1 Corinthians 11:18–19).

After Jesus ascended to heaven, the high priest and the Sadducees arrested the apostles and put them in prison for teaching in Jesus' name. Peter and the others, however, declared themselves witnesses to God's exaltation of Jesus and refused to recant. A respected teacher of the Law urged his fellow Israelites to release the apostles on the possibility that God may be supporting their efforts. The leaders decided it would do more harm than good to excommunicate them (Acts 5:17–42).

There are three formal ways for a believer to become separated from the visible Church: heresy, apostasy, and schism.

Heresy is the formal denial of a defined doctrine of the faith. With excommunication a baptized person is forbidden to receive the sacraments.

Apostasy is different from heresy. The early Church considered apostasy one of the unpardonable sins, along with murder and fornication. It is the complete abandonment of Christianity. An apostate is one who defects from the Church and is separated by willful choice from its life.

Schism is a deliberate separation from the unity of the Church. Unlike heresy it is not primarily a separation over a doctrinal issue but is a severing of communion. Although the Catholic Church still considers those out of communion with Rome to be schismatic, particularly those who separated from Rome at the time of the Reformation, the Second Vatican Council declared that anyone baptized into another communion is in "some, though imperfect, communion with the Catholic Church" *(Decree on Ecumenism*, #3).

The Church is visible above all when we can see the love of its members, one for another. Love is not an invisible feeling. It is a visible action on the part of one person for another. It is the giving of a cup, the sharing of a coat. It is fraternal correction. Where love is, God is there.

THE INVISIBLE CHURCH

As visible as it is, the Church is also invisible. Its divine life breathes with the freedom of the Spirit. Even the Church's sacraments and decrees celebrate God's grace but do not limit it. The Second Vatican Council makes clear that God's grace is universal (cf. *The Church in the Modern World*, #22). Jesus told the woman at the well that a time would come when true worship would no longer be on the mountain or in Jerusalem because "true worshipers will worship the Father in spirit and truth, for . . . God is spirit" (John 4:21–24).

This is why the Church is reluctant to excommunicate one of its members. Excommunication forbids one from receiving the sacraments but does not touch the hidden place in the human heart where the person relates to God. It is possible for the Church to excommunicate someone who nevertheless continues to enjoy God's grace.

Grace is the invisible, supernatural assistance that God gives to us for our sanctification. It is given freely, and we cannot earn it by our good works, nor do we deserve it through our prayers. The whole activity of divine life in the Church is a function of God's generous invisible grace. The sacraments are the normal way for God's grace to be conveyed in the Church, but God's grace exists even in those who have not been baptized.

We are said to be in the state of sin when through the effects of original sin or through our own actual sins we turn ourselves away from the grace of God. Because grace is invisible we cannot presume to make judgments about any person's relationship with God. Such judgments belong to God alone.

6 The Church Is an Institution and a Living Organism

Institutions are powerful forces in the world. They influence people's lives and their lifestyles. They wield authority in commerce and government. They exert their control through a complex chain of command, with executives having authority over middle management, and with middle management having authority over lower-level staff.

Life in Christ is a life in spirit and in truth because God is spirit (John 4:23–24). That life is free to move where it chooses. As the gracious gift of God, it comes to us without obligation and sometimes by surprise. We cannot earn it or grasp it. We cannot keep it from people who seem unworthy of it. Nor can we restrict it or control it by our laws or our institutions. Not even our belief has power over it.

The Roman Catholic Church today is a powerful, worldwide institution. It exists to serve God and to proclaim the presence of Christ in the world through time.

THE EARLY CHURCH

In his first public statements Jesus calls his followers to repentance because the kingdom of God is near (Matthew 4:17, Mark 1:15, Luke 4:18–19). This was a call for conversion and renewal of life in a new age inaugurated by God. It demanded humility, vigilance, compassion, and a righteousness based not on law but on love.

As a community, the disciples were learning to give in the measure they were given, as Jesus had taught them. And to put their lamp on a lamp stand. To be like the seed falling into good soil to bring forth grain (Mark 4:1–34). To be merciful and poor in spirit. To be the salt of the earth, the light of the world, the least in the kingdom. To reconcile with their brother and sister before offering their gift at the altar. To turn the cheek, and to go the second mile. To give alms in secret and to store up treasures in heaven (Matthew 5–6).

From the beginning, the disciples thought of themselves as an organic society in the belief that they had inherited the promises God made to Israel. They were the community of Israel's hopes (Luke 16:19–31; Acts 2:21, 47; 3:25) and the new assembly of Israel (Acts 2:17–41; 5:11; 8:1, 3; 9:31; 11:22, 26). The Church based its claim on the Lord's teaching about the kingdom, on his choosing of the apostles for its ministry, and on his institution of the sacraments. By instituting these structures of prayer, leadership, and signs of spiritual life, Christ assured the Church that they were a living organism whose life came from God.

In the Gospels and the Letters of Paul, there is a strong emphasis on collaboration, charisms, and living in community. But in the later New Testament writings, such as the Letters to Titus and Timothy, we see a concern for the Church's organization and its institutional roles. The apostles began to exercise their gifts for teaching and miracles. They became leaders in the churches.

The relationship of the local churches to the church in Jerusalem illustrates that the distant church communities came to defer to the church in Jerusalem. Each of the local churches had an equal status, but they all looked to Jerusalem for their authority and unity. Meetings took place in Jerusalem to resolve disputes in the local churches.

The early Church also faced the kinds of problems typical of any institution—requirements for membership, organization and structure, and consensus in its beliefs.

This organization of living communities of believers has been the model for the institution of the Catholic Church ever since. Catholics belong to local churches, the individual parishes whose leaders are priests. They look to their bishop and the cathedral for their unity in Christ. And the bishops and the dioceses they oversee look to the bishop of Rome for their full authority and unity in the worldwide Church.

In order to build up the Church, Christ bestows living charisms of gifts. Each Christian is responsible for exercising his or her gifts and for fulfilling these and other duties for the upkeep of the Church, without intruding on the duties of others (1 Corinthians 12:28).

The Church designates officials of distinct rank to oversee the exercise of these gifts and ministries. It teaches that God established offices according to a set order: apostles first, then prophets, teachers, deeds of power, gifts of healing, forms of assistance, forms of leaders, and various kinds of tongues (1 Corinthians 12:28).

THE INSTITUTIONAL CHURCH TODAY

The institution of the Roman Catholic Church is headquartered in Vatican City, a tiny sovereign state located within the city of Rome. The total area of the Vatican is less than a fifth of a square mile.

The pope is the Vatican's head of state. In that capacity he attends to the temporal or "secular" matters of one of the world's smallest nations.

The Vatican has its own postal system and its own coinage, a bookstore, a clinic and pharmacy, an astronomical observatory, a daily newspaper, a fire department, a radio station, and a train station for the convenience of the pope. Some of its administrative offices are located within the Vatican, but many are located in Rome. The Vatican also has a world-class art museum, a renowned library, and the famed Sistine Chapel.

The pope is also the bishop of Rome. Like every bishop he has a cathedral. His cathedral is not St. Peter's Basilica in Vatican City but the Cathedral of St. John Lateran in Rome. As the bishop of Rome, the pope is the spiritual head of the worldwide Roman Catholic Church. He exercises spiritual duties over his diocese and over the entire Roman Catholic Church. He retains complete legal, executive, and judicial power in the Vatican, over both its temporal and its spiritual concerns. In official documents the pope is identified as the servant of the servants of God.

Because he is the bishop of Rome, the pope enjoys a privileged status in regard to all other bishops. In the same way that Christ singled out Peter from the other bishops, so his successors as the bishops of Rome are the visible source of unity for bishops and all the faithful. As such, the pope is the pastor of the Church and exercises "full, supreme, and universal power" over it (see *Catechism of the Catholic Church*, #882, 883). The pope's stature is similar to that of the leaders of the church in Jerusalem during New Testament times.

The Vatican receives ambassadors from other countries and is represented in other countries by papal legates or nuncios. The legate has considerable jurisdiction over the affairs of the Church in the country to which he is assigned.

The pope appoints cardinals to assist him in his administrative duties. The cardinals are ranked as princes, and they enjoy certain state privileges. They are the pope's immediate advisors, and they assume the government of the Catholic Church in the absence of a pope. The cardinalate is attached to the person of the pope himself, not to jurisdiction over the Church. Unlike the office of bishop, the rank of cardinal is not essential to the Church, nor were there cardinals in the apostolic age. Today, however, all cardinals are bishops and can be distinguished by their red cassocks, or black cassocks with red trim.

Cardinals ordinarily reside in Rome unless they are also bishops of foreign dioceses. The bishops of New York, Baltimore, St. Louis, and Chicago, for instance, are usually also made cardinals by the pope. The cardinals take charge of Vatican offices and chair ecclesiastical committees. When a pope dies, the cardinals meet in secret sessions in the Sistine Chapel to select one of their number to be the new pope. This privilege has belonged exclusively to the college of cardinals since 1179.

The English word "bishop" comes from the Greek word for "overseer." Bishops oversee that part of the Church entrusted to them. Their territory is called a diocese, and it includes any number of parishes or local churches to which Catholics in that area belong. The bishops' authority derives from that of the apostles and from Christ himself. The New Testament describes their role in the Church as of paramount importance.

The bishop's principal duties include the administration of the sacraments proper to him, especially confirmation and holy orders, and the general oversight of his diocese, particularly evangelization, catechesis, and the supervision of his clergy. In large dioceses the bishop may be assisted by other bishops subordinate to him.

An archbishop is a bishop in charge of an archdiocese. Besides administering his own diocese, an archbishop has certain provincial responsibilities toward the bishops of the neighboring dioceses as well.

Bishops are the highest order of ministers in the Church. The New Testament witnesses to the leadership of the Church by these overseers (Acts 20:28). Peter called for someone to take the place of Judas as an overseer in the Church (Acts 1:20). Paul identifies bishops as presbyters (Titus 1:5). There is no clear distinction between bishops and presbyters in the New Testament (Acts 20:17, 28). From the standpoint of Scripture, there are no leaders higher in rank than the bishop.

In the Roman Catholic Church, bishops are appointed by the pope, in consultation with the Vatican's Congregation for Bishops and others with whom the pope chooses to confer. In other Churches, such as the Episcopal Church in the United States, bishops are elected by lay and clerical representatives from the diocese. In the Church of England the officials of the cathedral and the diocese, as well as the reigning monarch, are responsible for the election of bishops.

The insignia of a bishop are the chair in the cathedral, the miter (a liturgical headdress), the crosier or pastoral staff, the pectoral cross, and the ring. The bishop wears a purple cassock or a black cassock with red trim.

One distinction between a bishop and a priest is that bishops have the power to confer the sacraments of holy orders and confirmation. In some circumstances today priests can confirm on behalf of the bishop. Priests cannot confer the sacrament of ordination. (For a more thorough discussion of the distinctions between a bishop and a priest, see *Catechism*, #1555–1561.)

In the New Testament, each local church was governed by a board of elders or presbyters. The New Testament does not make clear distinctions between overseers and presbyters. Some presbyters were also called overseers. Paul, for instance, addressed the presbyters of Ephesus as overseers (Acts 20:17, 28).

Later, however, bishops were clearly distinct from presbyters and shared their authority with them. Presbyters were authorized to administer in the Church, to teach, and to exercise priestly functions in union with their bishops. The English word "priest" is a contraction of the word "presbyter."

In the New Testament, however, the words "priest" and "priesthood" are never used specifically of Christian ministers. They are applied to the Christian body as a whole. The idea of a specific ministry of priests was a gradual development in the Church. Little by little, priests assumed many of the duties originally reserved to bishops. Priests serve as the pastoral leaders of individual parishes within the diocese. They are accountable to the bishop, and they exercise their ministry in collaboration with him. Priests regularly administer the sacraments of baptism, Eucharist, matrimony, reconciliation, and anointing of the sick. The stole is the liturgical vestment of those in holy orders. Priests wear the stole around their neck with the ends falling straight down in front. The priest's cassock is black, although its use in North America is rare today.

The word presbyter is the technical name for anyone ordained into the priesthood in the Catholic Church. The presbyterate is the collective ministry of priests under their bishop.

The Church's early need for deacons is clearly described in the New Testament. The apostles had received complaints that the widows were being neglected in the daily distribution of food. To alleviate the problem, they ordained seven members in good standing to serve as deacons (Acts 6:1–6).

Deacons serve the poor and the needy in various ways, and they represent the needs of the world before the congregation. Deacons often take responsibility for social justice programs in the parish and for other forms of outreach. In the parish the deacon is responsible to the pastor. The rank of deacon is below that of the priest.

In the liturgy, the deacon proclaims the Gospel, preaches, leads the general intercessions, administers communion, and assists the priest in other ways. The deacon may also baptize and officiate at burials when the Eucharist is not celebrated. Deacons cannot preside at Mass, absolve penitents from sin, or pronounce blessings.

Candidates for the priesthood are first ordained to the transitional diaconate. They remain deacons usually for a year and are then ordained priests. For many centuries no one was ordained a deacon for life.

The Second Vatican Council restored the permanent diaconate. In subsequent years thousands of men who have no intention of being ordained priests have been ordained deacons in the Church's ministry of service.

Because the diaconate is open to married men, deacon formation takes into account the circumstances of their family lives. The deacons' wives are often included in the formation process. In accordance with tradition, a deacon who loses his wife does not remarry.

The structure of the Church is not usually thought to include the order of the laity. There are many more laity in the Church, however, than there are popes, cardinals, bishops, priests, and deacons.

The Second Vatican Council sought to humanize the Church's imposing structures. The bishops assumed a more collegial role with the pope, the local church took on greater autonomy, parish councils were authorized to take on advisory roles with the pastor, and there was increased co-responsibility at all levels of the Church's life.

7 The Church Is Tradition and Prophecy

The voice of monasticism and of the active religious orders has long been a voice of prophecy in the Church. In the Middle Ages, St. Francis and St. Dominic inspired a spiritual rededication to simplicity of life and a reforming lifestyle. Through their complete poverty and their dedication to preaching, teaching, and missionary activities, they gave a prophetic voice to a Church in need of reform. Prophets are spokespersons for God, not for forecasting the future but for calling the people of God to justice, honesty, and truth.

The reforms in Counter-Reformation Catholicism were led by prophetic theologians like St. Robert Bellarmine, by new religious orders like the Jesuits who were founded by St. Ignatius of Loyola, and by saintly reformers like St. Teresa of Avila and St. John of the Cross. In our own day the Berrigan brothers, Thomas Merton, and Mother Teresa have been called voices of prophecy in the Church.

It is the task of the laity to bear prophetic witness in the world, because they are the Church's vanguard in the world. Through the encounter of their faith with the signs of the times, they are restless and eager to keep their faith responsive to the ethical challenges presented by life in the modern world.

With the Second Vatican Council, the Roman Catholic Church made some of the most profoundly prophetic statements in its entire history. Preparation for reform was under way for over half a century through the efforts of various popes, grassroots movements, and theologians committed to reform. The proposal to convene the council, however, came from Pope John XXIII, who attributed the idea to a sudden inspiration of the Holy Spirit.

The council opened in 1962, conducted four sessions, and ended in 1965. It produced 16 documents that set the course for some of the greatest reforms in the Church's history. The two most important documents are the *Dogmatic Constitution on the Church* and the *Pastoral Constitution on the Church in the Modern World.*

Prophecy has not always been welcome in a Church that looks to apostolic authority for its tradition. Indeed some bishops were quite opposed to some of the more prophetic utterances of the council.

Tradition in the Church is not the same thing as custom. It is not the lame defense that "we've always done it that way." Tradition is, rather, the revelation God made to his faithful people through the prophets and apostles. Its central facts are found in the creeds, and in the evidence of primitive Christian institutions and practices that confirm scriptural teaching.

It is through the tradition of faithful teaching, worship, and life that a person adopts a Christian identity in the world. The example of family and parish, and the exemplary lives of prophetic leaders in the faith, are the lived tradition into which we are baptized and grow to Christian maturity.

Prophecy is the means by which the Church can assess its faithfulness to the apostolic tradition. Tradition and prophecy together are vital and life-giving. One without the other leads to a distortion of the faith. The Church needs both in order to inherit the kingdom of God.

8 The Church Is the Body of Christ and the Community of Redeemed Sinners

When we receive holy communion, the priest or other minister says to us, "The Body of Christ" and "The Blood of Christ." We respond, saying "Amen." Then, in consuming the sacramental bread and wine, we take the Body and Blood of Christ into our body, mind, heart, and soul.

The Body of Christ, however, is not limited to the sacramental species of bread and wine. It exists in another important form. All who are baptized by water and the Spirit also make up the Body of Christ. St. Paul conceives of the Church as Christ's Body (Colossians 1:24), with Christ as the head of the Church, and the fullness of his life dispensed through the Church to all its members (Ephesians 1:22–23).

When Paul appealed for unity in the churches, he did so on the basis that the Church is the one Body of Christ. Division in the Church upsets the unity of the Body of Christ (1 Corinthians 12:12, Romans 12:4). The unity of the Body of Christ is symbolized by the one bread of the Eucharist (1 Corinthians 10:17). To the world, division in the Church looks like a breakdown of Christ himself. It is a scandal.

The notion of the Church as the Mystical Body of Christ was first discussed at the First Vatican Council in the nineteenth century. It was later presented to the universal Church by Pope Leo XIII in 1896. It reached its greatest impact through Pope Pius XII's encyclical letter *Mystici Corporis* in 1943. The full significance of the concept, however, had to wait until the Second Vatican Council. Catholics are discovering that even as laity, their membership in the Body of Christ is a privilege of royal, priestly, and prophetic magnitude.

Baptism, however, is no easy ticket to heaven. Even as members of the Body of Christ, we are a community of sinners in need of redemption. The privilege of membership demands constant reformation and conversion. Not until the Church is finally washed clean in the blood of the paschal Lamb will the Body of Christ on Earth be perfectly one with the ascended body of Christ in glory. That is the day we long for with joy.

9 The Church Is the Bride of Christ, the New Israel

Jesus called himself the bridegroom (Matthew 9:15, Mark 2:19, Luke 5:34), just as Hosea described God as the spouse of Israel bound to her by covenant (Hosea 2:2–23).

Likewise St. Paul conceived of the Church as the Bride of Christ (2 Corinthians 11:2, 1 Corinthians 12:27, Ephesians 5:32). Christ loves the Church and is its savior. Christ gives his own life on behalf of his bride. To refer to the Church as the Bride of Christ is to acknowledge our own obligation to be faithful.

Jesus loves the Church as a bridegroom loves his bride. A young bride and groom keep their union alive by sharing tokens of their love. They steal glances across a crowded room, give flowers on anniversaries, cover for each other in need, and share meals and their most intimate moments.

The sacraments and the word are glances between God and the Church, like the glances between a bride and groom. God speaks words of love and promise. The Church hears them, brings gifts of praise and repentance, and discovers them transfigured into the very likeness of God.

The Israelites referred to themselves as the assembly of Yahweh. It was this assembly of Israelites that was the beloved of God. Because the early Christians also referred to themselves as the assembly, or the ekklesia, of all who believed in Jesus Christ, they clearly saw themselves as the legitimate successor of the Bride of Israel.

St. Paul calls the members of the Church by a number of titles: saints, those who love God, those who are called (Romans 8:27), the Church of God, those who have been made holy (1 Corinthians 1:2), and the chosen holy ones of God (Colossians 3:12). These titles were all used of Israel in the Old Testament. They indicate that the Church thought of itself as the true Israel and the legitimate heir of the covenant promises.

The New Testament as a whole teaches that the Church was established by Christ to be the New Israel and was endowed as such by the Holy Spirit at Pentecost. The Church is not just a voluntary association of followers.

A popular hymn describes the union of Christ with the Church as a union of a bride and groom:

The Church's one foundation is Jesus Christ her Lord;
She is his new creation by water and the word:
From heaven he came and sought her to be his holy bride;
With his own blood he bought her, and for her life
he died.

10 The Church Is a Community of Prophets, Priests, and Kings

The Church has many words in its vocabulary that have their origins in cultures very different from our own. It takes hard work on our part to understand their significance for us.

When we hear, for instance, that baptism has made us prophets, priests, and kings, it is easy for us to ignore these words as quaint and poetic but archaic titles that have little relevance for us. With a little translation or interpretation, however, we find their meanings can turn a couch-potato Christian into a quarterback Christian.

We imagine prophets as scruffy, long-haired, anti-social rabble-rousers who sometimes tell the future. We think of priests as single men who run parishes and wear long dress-like clothes at Mass. We think of kings as wealthy monarchs with scarlet and white robes in their closets who rule countries that are not democracies. So how is the Church a community of prophets, priests, and kings?

As a prophet, every Christian has the power and the obligation to maintain a close contact with the word of God so as to speak forcefully on God's behalf in the world. This means we have to be well-acquainted with revelation as it comes to us through Scripture and the Church. It also means that we have no need to be afraid of the face-off between revelation and a sometimes contrary world. Baptism empowers us to confront the evil and injustice we encounter in our jobs, at school, and in the marketplace.

As a priest in Christ, every Christian has the power to improve the world's relationship with God through praise and sacrifice. Christ is the one and only high priest, whose offering of his body and blood on the cross turned the world around and brought us into friendship again with God. As baptized members of the Church, however, we participate in that same sacrifice when we join the totality of our own lives, the good as well as the bad, to the offering of Christ at Mass, so that God may be praised in everything. Thanks to our baptism in Christ, the surrendering of ourselves, our feelings, our minds, hearts, and even our bodies as a sacrifice for good, profoundly affects our relationship with God. Our sacrifice is not in vain. The New Testament testifies to the priestly character of the Church (1 Peter 2:9, Revelation 1:6, 5:10).

Through our kingship with Christ, every Christian is reborn into a realm of love, goodness, and light and enjoys a dignity that knows no distinction of persons and excludes no one. Christ assures us that there is no poverty or want, no weeping or sorrow in that kingdom, not for anyone who has been washed in the blood of Christ's sacrifice. The banquet table is plentiful, the singing glorious. In baptism all of us are kings with Christ, who is the King of all kings. The New Testament testifies to the royal character of the Church (1 Peter 2:9, Revelation 1:6, 5:10). Only in the Church is everyone a king by divine right.

11 The Church Is the Lay and Ordained People of God

The model of the Church as the people of God has successfully captured the attention of Roman Catholics since the Second Vatican Council. It was not a new idea. The New Testament described the followers of Christ as "a chosen race, a royal priesthood, a holy nation, God's own people" (1 Peter 2:9).

The church in Jerusalem was the parent and prototype of the other local churches. It enjoyed a primacy of the parent church and had its own hierarchy. The other churches were similarly organized, with their own bishops, presbyters, and deacons, and were founded by apostles.

St. Paul wrote that the Church was erected upon the foundation of apostles and prophets, with Christ himself as the cornerstone (Ephesians 2:20).

The ordained ministry of bishops, priests, and deacons have the duties of teaching the faith, leading the people in divine worship, principally the Eucharist, and guiding the whole Church as pastors. It is the task of the ministry of the ordained to prepare the laity to fulfill their task in the world.

The vocation of the laity is oriented toward the world's daily ordinariness: the school, commerce, the workplace, government, and to those in need. The laity grapple with the pressing issues of the day, and they interpret them with the mind of Christ. They do not avoid complicated moral dilemmas raised by science and technology but rather educate themselves so as to make responsible Christian choices. They work toward the betterment of the world, for its justice and for peace. They share in the world's pains and joys. They engage heartily in all human activities that are consistent with the mind of Christ, often in collaboration with other Churches and organizations with which it is not in full agreement on all issues. The lay Catholic who once lived in a clear-cut world of black and white now lives in a world of shades of gray.

As the people of God, Catholics make the most of the present day, they involve themselves in culture and government, they express their Christian hope within the realm of secular society, and they interpret the signs of the times. They value the dignity and freedom of all people everywhere. They are fully citizens of the world. The Second Vatican Council declared that everything said of the people of God applies equally to the laity, religious, and clergy.

12 The Church Is the Heavenly City on Earth

When St. Paul told the Christians at Ephesus that they were citizens with the saints, he was using an analogy (Ephesians 2:19). He was comparing the Church to a city, and he described the members of the Church as its citizens, who were entitled to all the rights and duties of citizenship. In the Greek world of Paul's day, cities were built around the marketplace, and they included public baths, a theater, and a stadium. The city government was conducted by a senate and an assembly (ekklesia) of the people. Before the advent of modern nationhood, the city was the most important jurisdiction to which a citizen belonged.

In the Old Testament, as in the ancient Near East generally, a city was a walled and fortified enclosure. Cities were very small by our standards. They ranged from 6 or 7 acres to perhaps 15, with few cities being as large as 20 acres. Cities were built where there was a source of water and where they could be defended from attack. They were crowded and densely populated, with roughly 50 people per acre. There were no wide streets as we know them today but only narrow passageways winding between rows of houses. The streets were not paved. The few open spaces were located at the gates to the city.

In the ancient world as well as in the modern world, the life of the city represents the full attainment of human aspiration. It symbolizes civilization and culture. At least in principle, its wealth is plenty for all. The city represents the goal of human striving.

A fortified city has similarities to a garden paradise. Both are safe, comfortable places because both are walled in by protective enclosures. In their ancient origins the words "paradise" and "garden" both implied being walled about, like an oasis surrounded by wasteland. Even though an enclosed garden courtyard may be small, we don't feel confined by it. We enjoy the serenity of its well-tended pathways and the gurgle of its flowing fountains. It is a haven of peace.

Running streams keep the desert out of the walled paradise, just as four rivers flowed from Eden, watering all the green trees and plants in the garden. The garden produces everything that is pleasant to see and good to eat. It is beautiful and prosperous. It is a place to rest away from the heat of the sun and to repose in the cool shade.

THE CITY OF GOD

The Hebrews thought of the fortified city of Jerusalem as the city of God. The Lord's Temple stood in the city. The Israelites knew that all the abundance that made possible the building of the Lord's house came from God's own hand (1 Chronicles 29:14–16). They knew that it was only as secure as God chose to make it. After the destruction of the city, the prophets inspired a messianic hope in the rebuilding of Jerusalem from its ruins. In its restoration, the prophets described Israel as the garden of Eden replanted by the Lord. In the garden Israel would know joy and gladness, and her song would be one of thanksgiving (Isaiah 51:3, Ezekiel 36:35).

Christians thought of the earthly Jerusalem as a type of the heavenly Jerusalem. It is the city of the living God, where innumerable angels are gathered in festive assembly (Hebrews 12:22). Christians belong not to any earthly city but are the citizens of this heavenly Jerusalem (Philippians

3:20). The city is yet to come (Hebrews 13:14), and it comes out of heaven, from God (Revelation 3:12).

St. John, the traditional writer of the Book of Revelation, describes the heavenly city as shining with precious stones. Its 12 gates are always open, day and night. The city has no temple because God is its temple. There is no sun or moon because the glory of God illuminates the city. No one unclean enters the city (Revelation 21–22).

The heavenly Jerusalem represents the Christian belief that in the city of God we shall attain the fulfillment of all our needs and all our yearning. Suffering and grief will end, and night will be as day.

Many hymnals contain the hymn that has this first stanza about the new Jerusalem:

O holy city, seen of John,
Where Christ, the Lamb, doth reign,
Within whose foursquare walls shall come
No night, nor need, nor pain,
And where the tears are wiped from eyes
That shall not weep again!

THE CHURCH'S VISIONARY SENSE

In the apostolic age, the Church expected Christ to return again quickly (Matthew 24–25, Mark 13, Luke 21). Paul had to remind the various churches to live blameless lives in readiness for the Lord's return. They would have little warning that the time was near (1 Thessalonians 4–5, 1 Corinthians 15). It never occurred to the disciples that the Church might last for thousands of years.

Even with the Church now firmly planted in time, its vision is nevertheless still trained on the end of the world. With a prevailing sense of advent, the Church conducts all its affairs under the gaze of eternity, waiting for the consummation of time and space. Its worship, its mission, and its daily living have the expectant sense that they are temporary. When we look at the Church's work and worship, we enjoy a glimpse of what the kingdom will look like at the end of time (Matthew 11–13).

Through its visionary senses, the Church looks at bread and wine but sees the Body of Christ in glory. It looks at a church and sees not the building but the eternal Church of God in victory. It looks at the world's poor and impoverished and sees the beloved of God. In other words, the Church lives in the world knowing that creation is not finished and that the last day of creation will come only on the eighth day, the day of resurrection, when all will be taken with Christ into glory. That is why St. Paul urged the saints to set their minds on things that are above, not on things that are on Earth (Colossians 3:2).

The Church is thus the fortified garden-city of the community of the redeemed. Within its sturdy enclosures the saints are bathed in cleansing streams and fed on the fruit of God's word. There is abundance and peace for all, and security within its walls. The powers of hell will not prevail against this city, nor will death subdue it. Paul reminded the Corinthians that even if their earthly dwelling place is destroyed, they have a building from God, a house not made with hands, eternal in the heavens (2 Corinthians 5:1). In the fortified garden-city of the Church, the saints will see the face of God.

The city's fortifications are not designed to isolate the saints from the world or to protect them from its suffering. For the sake of the city of God, they may be hungry and thirsty, poorly clothed, homeless, and weary (1 Corinthians 4:11). The city, however, frees them to work with Christ in transforming the earthly city into the eternal city of God.

The walls strengthen us so that we are certain to survive whatever engagements we make with the powers of darkness and death. We address God from the security of the garden-city: "Lord, you have been our dwelling place in all generations" (Psalm 90:1).

In the words of the popular mission song:

Let us build the city of God.
May our tears be turned into dancing!
For the Lord, our light and our love,
has turned the night into day!